CSU Poetry Series XXVI

WHEN
I KEPT
SILENCE

Naomi Clark

Cleveland State University Poetry Center

ACKNOWLEDGMENTS

The author is grateful to the National Endowment for the Arts for a Creative Writing Fellowship and to Centrum Foundation, Port Townsend, Washington, for a residency which helped make this collection possible; and to the editors of the following journals, in which some of the poems first appeared (some in earlier versions or under different titles):

BOTTOMFISH: "From a Prison Drawing by Valente Malangatana"

CIMARRON REVIEW: "The Language of Doors"

NIMROD: "The Crow-Feather," "Charles L. Broley, Champion Eagle Bander, Talks of Eagles: Hard Times," "Broley Talks: The Eyrie (1)," and "The Crow Tree"

PRAIRIE SCHOONER: "Believing Water: In the Time of Famine"

QUARRY WEST: "Thomas Aquinas," "Thou Art My Rock," "Bones," "In Whose Sprit There Is No Guile," "The Congregation," "Remembering a Child Who Died of Whooping Cough: Bamako, Mali," and "The Fish"

"Son of the Morning" appeared in an earlier version under a different title in *Burglaries and Celebrations*, by Naomi Clark (Berkeley: Oyez Press, 1977, Copyright © by Naomi Clark, 1977).

For information and some quotations used in "The Kingdom," I am indebted to George Laycock's book, *Autumn of the Eagle* (New York: Scribners, 1973), and to the eagle banders whose reports he cites; especially Charles L. Broley, whose character I have fictionalized somewhat by merging with his reports those of other banders Laycock cites, and by attributing to him my own observations and imaginings. "The Eyrie (1)" is almost a found poem. — N.C.

Funded Through
Ohio Arts Council

727 East Main Street
Columbus, Ohio 43205-1796
(614) 466-2613

This book is for my family:
Burnie,
Diane, David, Joel,

and for
Robert

CONTENTS

I. BELIEVING WATER

KILLING PUPS

I am afraid to tell you.

We need a man to kill them,
they said. I counted:
twelve dogs, three pregnant,
three in heat, one nursing five pups;
half-wild cats, shadows too quick to number.
All dumped. Always hungry.
My mother ill, the two women hungry,
the money we'd sent spent on pet-food.

I took three pups in my arms.
They sucked my fingers,
squealed like little pigs, nuzzled my breast;
pushed with their paws against my ribs.
I put them in a box, took shovel and hammer,
in the fallow garden dug a hole.

I had not thought they could struggle so.
They wriggled in my hands, blind
eyes, blind noses searching.
The sharp, soft claws of their toes
scratched the skin of my wrists.

Square in the dome of the forehead
I hit the first,
my whole weight behind the arm,
and the second, and they squealed,
convulsed, fought, and I hit them again,

again, and shovelled as fast
as I could. As dirt fell,
one fought awake, pushed at the clods.
I stomped the full hole solid,
took the third pup back in the house.

The males don't eat much, my mother said.
We'll keep them for watchdogs, my sister said.
Thank you, they both said, thank you, thank
you, you're very brave.

I took the females to the vet,
paid for lethal injections.
The kids could go barefoot,
as I did and their father.

THE FLIES

They walk on such slender arms, such
finely articulated hands.
This one carefully cleans mouth-parts,
joints of the neck, mosaic eyes,
a stretched gauze wing.

He's fat, nose like a stinger,
green when sun hits the black torso,
bronze and green.

On the farm, I saw all colors, sizes,
clouds of perfectly replicated infants.
Flies that could hide
the head of a pencil
drew blood, stampeded
the horses, made me cry
my first curses.
Flies crawled in layers on screen doors.
Crawled our sleep.
Blackened uncovered food. Screwworms
twisted in sores on cows' backs,
in what for a few days the coyotes
missed of a cow's carcass;
after Dad smashed the old cat's head,
in the unlicked eyes of kittens.

When the rattler bit Queenie,
she scratched the swelling near her ear
and the flies came. I held her,
the boys poured on stock dip.

The blowfly grubs hatched anyhow,
ate dead flesh to the brain,
half the brain as it died, before
I'd let Paul shoot her.

Hissed under the outhouse seat,
diving and surfacing like turtles.
The stench burned the nose.
I chose, summers when the heat made
it all worse, the far row of the garden,
till Mother saw and switched me.

From those seas of their birth
the flies came,
straight to the kitchen, the milk bucket,
the cows' teats and my mother's,
fruit drying on the roof,
the company table spread on Sundays.
Spray, molasses paper.
Fly swatters in every room,
my job to use them,
my aim no better than
a cross-eyed pig's.

It's rare to see one now,
blue-bottle against the window,
the whine in a lighted room,
food black. I look
at a green fly in the sun,
at a garden where with a million others
I crawled out of the belly of the first corpse,
burst my skin, dried wet wings, rose,
innocent as matter, into the bold light.

THE CONGREGATION

When we arrived at the football field
before Easter dawn,
carrying ragged forsythia, loudspeakers,
the Girls' Auxiliary flag, the Cross,
all the bleachers were filled with crows.
They walked up and down the benches,
gathered in small groups,
laid their tracks
in rippled mounds heaped up by spring sandstorms.
Across the wide stretch of sand and dry grass,
they called companionably.
We hammered on the bottoms of communion trays.
The crows flew up,
a beating of black wings and voices.
As the sun and the sermon rose,
they lifted their noise unto the Lord.
I wanted to speak in tongues, but all I could
say was "Caw, caw, caw," and I kept that
low in my throat.

That night, moon low in the west, I
climbed out my window, went back.
The crows were there.
They hardly woke up as they made room
for me, cawing softly in their sleep.

When the sun rose, nobody came,
and all around me the crows flew up,
beating their wings like cymbals,

lifting their black voices in the empty air
high, higher, away over the dry pastures
and the oil pumps, toward Oklahoma,
toward new green shoots, corn
just breaking the soil of Kansas.

THE LANGUAGE OF DOORS

for Burnie

Once, grubbing out stumps, you
gashed a snake—I want you to
remember. You brought it to me,
silver-grey with a coral belly,
necklace, smooth rounded jaw.
The flesh of the snake's side,
torn, showed white.
The slow cold blood mixed with dirt.
The snake twisted, doubled,
redoubled its shining length,
grey over coral, coral over grey.
You put it in my hands.
Against my breastbone I held it
till it lay quiet and still.
You cleaned the wound,
led me down the slope,
lifted the stump.
We laid the snake where as it slept
the steel had caught it:
to die in its own place.

A year later, working the firebreak,
you turned over a log,
called me to see a snake,
silver-grey with a coral belly,
coral necklace;
where the gash had been,
a scar like braided leather.

The snake coiled round my arm,
tasted the air as I lifted it,
ducked under my shirt,
climbed my breastbone.

I know a man jealous
of everything his wife touched,
his own body, her poems, doors
that swung outward or inward.

You, who when we came here hated
and feared all snakes,
turned the log back; you'd leave it.
We placed the snake
where a crook in the wood made a door.
Slowly, we learn a difficult language.

GOOSE

The yellow goose lies on her back in the dust.
She stretches her neck into the garden.
Her beak first was lopped short,
then mashed. It's healed.
She wriggles it into the small
spaces of the wire fence. She stretches
and pokes it into the kitchen window.
Her wings clipped, she lies
down in the dust of the yard,
wriggles her orange feet in air as once
she waved them in water.
That scarred tail—
it wriggles in dust.

At night when a yellow path
ripples and flicks over the lake,
a child travels in a goose boat.
Our family boat—a flat-bottomed
daytime box Dad hammered together
and, using Mother's old mop,
covered with tar—moved, a mastodon,
through shallow water. It always leaked.
The night boat
with its fat belly and goose shape
loved water, glided smooth and
crazy over black water.

Clown on land,
in water or in air the goose
moves in perfect grace.
My brother loved that long neck,

the orneriness of the beak. The yellow goose
chased me through the barnyard many a
morning, nipping my bare heels.
Nobody ate the yellow goose.
My mother hated her,
but she died of old age.

AN ELEGY FOR ABBY

> *The eyes of your understanding being
> enlightened* . . . .
>
> —Ephesians 1:18

1. Not the concept but the arm's movement,
    crow in a pine tree cawing,
    Spanish proverbs floating in sea air,
    coarse jokes in American. Car doors slam.
    Brewer's Blackbirds strut the pavement,
    their whistles trilled against orange
    lichen on the landside of the cypress.
    Young men in wetsuits cross the bright
    beach, leap black clusters of kelp.
    Far off the slow surf
    makes long strokes across the blue.
    Abby hears sea lions bark.
    Her brush hesitates, dips, turns;
    smell of coffee and woodchips.
    Far out, spouts of three whales.
    The sea moves. *No comprendo.*
    Yo no comprendo.

2. When Abby closed her mother's eyes,
    she saw them open for just one more look.
    She gave away her chalks,
    all the fine papers, brushes, paints.
    "There's time for one subject only,"
    she said; for her, one art.
    Her poems were gifts to any
    who could listen. She made a path
    for light to last beyond the end.

A gift begins a circle.
Like the motion of a wave the gift moves
one hand to another;
the circle as it opens
inward opens outward, its dance returning
from round the world
to sway the giver with new music.
To close the gift's circle
is to swallow one's own poison.
To fall, skin purple and black,
into the common well.
For a thousand years
men will turn from that water.

3. This morning, hardly visible among new oak leaves
   tiny green-yellow wild canaries sang.
   I heard the first calls of the small grey bird
   who comes to us only in early summer
   and all day long for weeks sends along the ridge
   a false hawk's shrill.
   Two male Lazuli Buntings in full
   flight from one song to another
   struck my window. I held their shining bodies,
   warm, limp, the feet already nearly stiff,
   the lapis blue of the back feathers
   against undergrey and white wing-bars
   the exact shade of wonder and longing
   I heard in your voice when in the old wood church
   you read your newest lines.

Your hand, Purple Martin of that
air off the cliff above the point's lighthouse,
marks the beat and flow of your voice.
You put your fingers in Christ's side,
the jagged curves, where through your body
the shotgun now has forced its final *no*.
You knew death would not let you go.
Yo no comprendo.
Though your voice shook in your throat
and all your bones shook,
to any who could receive them you gave
feathers you found on the beach,
shells, light from the cloud
where you saw the bird whose beak
would grip your neck,
who would be satisfied with nothing less than all.

WHERE, O LORD, IS THY VOICE?

*The light shineth in darkness; and the
darkness apprehendeth it not.*
—John 1:5

God in the rock,
in the oak,
in the blast to the chest
of the dearest friend.
God in her speech:
to be translated, the heart
torn apart, heart's blood scattered,
the word, the word.
God in starved bodies.
One nail, she said, *soaked
to rust, for a whole village*!
would give to the blood that
heart-dark hue. God
in the instruments of torture.
God in the adult
mad with desire to violate the child.
God in the cells
and in the cells gone wild.
God in the hand that held the gun.
God in my hand. God in her choice:
to make the word. Where, O Lord,
when the word was made flesh were you?
Her flesh is word now, Lord, is word.

BELIEVING WATER:
IN THE TIME OF FAMINE

When I watch moving water, I watch
always for the end of its flowing,
for the rush to slow,
rocks, water-weeds, mud to emerge,
the last thin stream like spilled memory
to hurry past and away,
or like water in the jar I broke
to disappear into sand,
the harvesters angry, my throat dry.

My mother, year after year her belly big,
through burning Texas summer and dry northers
carried water in buckets up a long hill.
Later, we drove the old horse
into muddy water;
the barrels filled, he strained and balked;
beaten, he struggled, got the sledge moving again,
under the lash dragged it home.
Each August black muck cracked deep,
the channel dried to a thin, dirty ribbon.
Seven children bathed in the same scummed water.

Dry gullies, washes, wells,
creek beds, river beds, lake beds
—more than ever I could see of live water.
Fish gasp, the last moisture returned to its source.
Springs diverted, no pools for the deer.
Foxes, even skunks go rabid.
The carcasses eaten, the crows fly.

Armadillos rot in their shells.
Women and men die in the asylum, so dry
the county gets by with a child's coffin.
Children stunted and gnarled, scaly as snakes.

I want to believe in water.
Tahoe City to Truckee, now,
the raft bus runs all day.
The river echoes with shouts and laughter.
No Vacancy signs stay up all season.
I watch the highway toward the casinos;
the ripples of that current never soften.

Where silver water pours over a rock,
white water bubbles uphill.
Crawdads, orange as those clouds
low in the west, grow big as lobsters here,
their round eyes clear in the crystal water.
Young men in tennis shorts
stand knee-deep in the shallows,
casting for keepers.
All across broad water meadows,
ponds reflect sky.
On the far side, darkness stills the rapids.
Even in drought year the Truckee lulls us.

In the moving rivers of images
before and behind my eyes,
wanderers seek the last small pool.
Families disappeared, tribes lost in sand.
Wealth drained away,

not to the cycling source;
to a gambler's forever,
to my own house,
to the table laid with crystal and silver.

II. WHEN I KEPT SILENCE

When I kept silence, my bones waxed old
through my roaring all the day long.

—Psalms 32:3

The poems in this section are dedicated to
William Everson.

THOMAS AQUINAS

He wanted to make a life so holy
crows would firk his bones clean.
Charles of Anjou poisoned him.
Through the weeks of his agony,
monks kept a fire high in the hearth.
His soul shriven, his breath gone,
monks dropped the body into the boiling pot.
With long forks they turned and flaked it.
Next day they fished out the bones,
bare, full of grace, saleable.

To kings and scholars,
he'd said: *We understand less than a pauper.*
Beyond reason, the crows wait.
When to your hunger a child brings a bone,
broken, polished by wind or teeth,
even a sliver, gnaw, grind it, swallow.

THOU ART MY ROCK

Farmers in Oxfordshire string crows on fenceposts.
They hang, a warning,
heads bowed aside,
wings spread to the nails.
Between Putnam and Cisco how many
coyotes nailed to the posts?
I counted. It was a game: one-hundred-and-one.

My brother, lost in drought on the Texas plain,
ate a dead crow raw.
The worst thing, he said, I have ever tasted.
Like death. Like eating my own body nine days de
Home, alive, he said it.

At dawn crows in the hemlocks begin their cries.
As the tide goes out, they drop,
raising through fog like Easter hymns
their joy. Sea cucumber! Crab!
Fledgling fallen from the high cliff nesthole!
Seal's carcass cast on the rocks!
Lift up your voices!

IN WHOSE SPIRIT THERE IS NO GUILE

I've seen crows peck apart
hard mud walls of those brown
gourds full of crying beaks,
seen crows' beaks with one blow
crack a bald skull
or firk up alive and torn
two naked infants, their blind
eyes unseared, unhouseled.
Each gash opens a raw wound.

The coydog, nose buried
in the belly of a road-killed fawn,
licks Christ's bones.
I eat flesh.
We gnaw out the marrow.

BONES

Nobody knows what happened to the old judge
Three months later we found his bones,
down in the last gully butts up at the Caprock.
Crows love anything shiny.
Jaw was still on the skull, open,
crows working harder than
woodpeckers to loosen the gold.
Two teeth gone already. Never did find them.
When Garrett came home from the war,
he said he'd seen crows pecking skulls like that
"Looking for what we missed," he said.

WITH MY SOUL HAVE I DESIRED THEE

From a rock on the cliff's edge
we watched the moon rise late,
turn the ridge-top silver-grey,
shadows of lateral ridges stark black.
We saw deer then, browsing on oak leaves;
raccoons silver and black moved from one
spot of light to another through leaves' shadows;
a fox watched us from another rock.
Even then: *I want to die.*

All earth's sentient inhabitants have been property.
Freed, believed myself property.
Cried out
through nights when the crows slept,
I want to die.

The pull to be owned:
arms of the father, the mother;
corporation, army, the great last fire.
That's the manatee sings us to war: *I want to die.*
Who shall protect the world against us?

SON OF THE MORNING

Last night an emperor hawk came to me,
golden-green as chrysoprase,
his eye a topaz:

in a landscape of prickly pear and mesquite
I stand still as a lone dead oak.
Golden-green as earliest February mesquite leaves
he preens and shimmers,
ruffles his feathers, stretches one wing,
bites at the bark where I broke away mistletoe.
He stretches his neck, takes a green cicada.

Looks at me, changes to a bird of painted tin,
of bottle shards, sequins, mica,
eye a grain of Indian corn,
talons dried cat's-claw sticks.

Looked at my white eyes,
changed to a cow-country lady's plaything.

Today, four Brewer's Blackbirds,
a Bullock's Oriole, a California Mocker
are chasing the biggest crow I've seen.
He'd settled on top of the telephone pole;
black, shining, folded his wings.
The little birds squawked.
The mockingbird dived.
The crow shakes his head at them.
From behind, the oriole pecks him.
Striped wings beat in his face.

Even the sparrows are gathering,
the finches brave as hornets.
Crow, black gleam on the telephone pole,
eye black as your feathers,
in this backyard you've caused
a great commotion;
hardly more could a peacock, should he stalk
and scream through onions and rhubarb,
trail his brocaded tail over lawn chairs;
hardly more the shadow of a hawk.
You we don't understand. As you lope
out of the window's frame, the wings that
brought you down the longest arc
flap slowly. In our terror
for once united,
we pursue you.

AT THE RUIN OF AN ARMY
BARRACKS ABOVE FORT WORDEN

We asked you for fish, Father.
You gave us the corpses of children.
We asked you, Father, for bread.
You gave us long guns
snaked out across water;
concrete bunkers
planted over with sweet peas and roses;
cloud, fire
rising above melted cities.

Rotten wood crumbles in my hand.
I taste the crumbled bread.
Grainy in my mouth,
the excrement of worms awakens me.

FROM A PRISON DRAWING
BY VALENTE MALANGATANA

1. Black body in a black cell,
   white eye at the door-hole spying.

   As the cell shrinks, his bones grow.
   "Out of heartwood of ebony,"
   he writes in the dark, "I dreamed a tree."

   The flesh goes. Everything
   goes but his eye's light.
   Against black walls an image forms.

   In the black cell, with no blade,
   from dirt and urine he shapes a tree.

   Carves it with nails and teeth.
   Against cheek, belly, palm, teeth,
   smooths the rough wood.

   "This tree cracks rock," he says.
   "This tree cracks walls."

   He plants it under the sack where
   once he slept.
   Now he does not sleep.

   As he goes out,
   from every cell a throat-hum rises.

2. Men with skin like mine, women with skin
   like mine; Dutch hymns, English ivy, guns, walls.

Under American sun, Black slaves, Indian slaves,
Irish slaves. Rows so long no one could count.
My father raged when I asked if he'd ever

seen a lynching; raged worse when my sister said
she'd marry a Black man if she wanted.

All walls crack, *Broeders*.
All hymns fail, Sisters. What
will we do if your skins burn black in the street?

A Black woman tells me: "I helped you
because you're human." Mary TallMountain

gives me her book and a pebble. "Suck it,"
she says, "for courage."

Sata trusted me with her baby.
Something under skin, under stone,
where blood cannot reach, does not fail.

The tree planted in a cell sends down roots,
roots out under walls, up. Those roots sprout.

THE CROW TREE

For the crows it's always Christmas,
their tree a tall old maverick pine
or a dead fir, its shining ornaments
their own black bodies. Thickly
they line the branches, silent;
peck the polished cone of a neighbor's beak.
Awake, they welcome no visitors;
huddle against change, shove, quarrel.
In black swarms they fly up, cawing,
swirl over cliff and water; settle,
on their high candelabrum
a new constellation.
A Great Blue Heron, ignoring them,
flaps, jeered like any angel,
and like any angel stiffens his wings,
shows their scope in a long curve,
eases his feet into the water,
waits for small fish. Matthew,

Mark, Luke, nor John tells us how,
when Christ's body was borne away to the cave
and the soldiers raised the cross
again under the black clouds and the lightning,
dropped its stump into the hole and hurried off,
the crows in their battalions ignored the stinking
     thieves,
fought for a place on the bare tree.

How the dominant male, as always,
preempted the central post.

How the outcast adolescents
pecked berries from the discarded crown.
Nor how crows had circled the manger,
crying for corn,
how Mary found a black feather,
saved it for the child to wear in his hair.

Here, even on foggy days the crows
light the fir's bones with their dark gleam.

III. CLOSEST TO VIRGO

CROW CHILD

A plague of crows fell out of a dull sky.
The year I was born, my mother told me,
they dug up seed, pulled sprouts;
from a bushel of seed potatoes, from a whole
litter of orphaned pigs pecked the eyes.
They sat, a solid row on the roof peak,
cawed down the stovepipe, rose up cawing
over the orchard, cursed the hard peaches
that they might ripen, jabbed sores
on dog's ears, pecked scabs from the rumps of hens.
Finches and wrens, cardinals
chased crows all day.

One night my mother met herself on a path:
a tree, an old oak, nearly dead.
Crows snuggled against her neck,
like cats rubbed their sleek black
over her jaws; over her breasts
spread shining wings.
On the bare wood of her fingers
they sharpened their beaks.
Her belly grew; six children
already she'd borne, six sleek mallard ducks.
Against the shrinking water from which she drank
they turned their wise heads, emerald, iridescent.
For her it was a time of cursed numbers:
she turned thirty-nine;
this child would be her seventh.
Her belly grew heavy; she feared
what she carried.

It was the year of failed banks,
exhausted gushers, of winds;
of smothering clouds—black dust
down from the high plains;
no work for a carpenter.
The sky burned, burned all day.
Lightning and thunder boiled no rain;
tornadoes whipped the horizon with their tails.
Crows gobbled the last of the stunted fruit.
Her husband beat the starved cattle,
kicked the old horse lame,
cursed her, cursed all her children.

Crows we have always with us,
she whispered to the dead cardinal
she'd fed from her hand.
Driving the cows home from pasture,
she met the black king of Hades,
boots, Stetson, slim pants, muscled shirt,
holster, guns blazing, all black.
As the sun rose, she beheld him judge,
black robes among white flames.
Noon, she beheld him a rodeo clown
riding black bulls in the prison arena at Huntsvil

The child, she said,
will be male,
his sex guarded by gleaming black feathers,
his fingers black flight quills, his eyes
so black no brother could find them.
With that black beak he can
eat whatever there is to eat.

My mother's labor took her
as she gathered the last of the pecked corn.
She lay down in the furrow.
Her great-grandmother, twelve years old,
small brother under her brown skirt,
while Comanches burned barn and home,
had lain too in a field of corn.
Later, a saint in Indian Territory,
she taught hymns and sums to the heathen;
despised and rejected,
came back with the Comanche she married,
planted an orchard in Comanche County.
In those defeated skies no eagles flew,
and she bore him no son.
For his daughter's hair, blonde as a Swede's,
he chose the crow's feathers.
Lying between the corn rows, my mother
imagined her own auburn hair
black as any Comanche's.
As my head crowned, a dull rain
broke over the field.

When I came out—a daughter!—
my mother cursed the crows and wept.
Her blood and her cries, she said,
next season, though the drought returned,
made the corn strong.
She tried for years, she said,
to lure a young crow into a cage for me,
to hatch a crow's egg under a hen.
She gave me a rooster like no fowl we'd seen,
saddle and over-feathers orange, gold, red.
She brought me many black feathers.

I have gone down into Hades, Mother.
You were not there,
the black king was not there.
Here on the beach of a mountain lake
I dance with crows. In any city
as they peck garbage in parking lots
I caw with them.
That is enough, Mother.

LISTENING TO RECORDED LOVE POEMS

Near Kasilof, the summer after the Alaska Quake,
trumpeter swans floated among acres of pink lilies,
hardly stirring the water.

A moose in deep water,
swimming the channel beyond our rented dock,
moved as though he'd climb a steep hill
or, risen on his hind legs,
would fight or mate.

His broad shoulders and breast
raised a bow wave and left a wake.
He lifted his heavy horns.

Each evening before twilight,
our only night,
the swans flailed their wings,
strode over the water.
Once we heard their clear horn-notes.
As they flew, a long arrow
west over the husky farm,
the dogs barked after them,
after their shadows.

The moose came out of the woods each morning.
At noon drops from his muzzle lay
silver on the dark green pads.
While David pulled in the big
Dolly Vardens and Rainbows,
day after day Diane sat in the boat
knitting among those lilies.

For days Joel spoke only to loons,
as loons call. Burnie, slim,
hard-muscled, moved between carefully kept
nineteenth-century machines,
among salmon flashing silver into bins
and down a long river of women's hands.
High tides washed over the sunken roadways.
At Anchorage houses lay,
smashed toys in a child's sandbox,
bulldozed gravel
flat over sunken shops and bodies.

A black bear—tall for his kind,
streaked auburn and brown,
his red tongue stained purple,
on a bog near the cannery
pushed aside the blueberry bushes.
We backed slowly away, clanging our buckets.
Raising his arms, he watched.
His fur glistened.
When Burnie came to our bed at midnight,
I pressed my face in the hair of his chest.

Today, in the car, in a hurry,
I listened: mist and the movement of water,
moose, a great bear, God's one-eyed horse.
Laughing, I forgot my hands on the wheel.
Two miles down Skyline in the wrong direction
driving almost atop the San Andreas,
I turned back, toward the freeway called

"Blood Alley." Robins and
forty-nine waxwings flew up.
In the rear-view mirror I saw them—
  scarlet wing-spots and rusty
  robins' breasts among the madrone's
  yellow, rust, scarlet berries—
  saw them settle again to eat,
  saw them eating, eating the berries.

MICE

1. When I held my first child, a daughter,
   and nursed her, my breasts full of pain,
   I was afraid. Like a kitten's paws
   her small hands pushed at the pulsing veins.
   What did I know of babies, or love, or myself?
   I sang to her, and a small mouse,
   its dark eyes wide open, came
   each time to stand up at the edge of the rug, swaying.

2. I heard the trap snap shut.
   The mouse who lived under the sofa,
   caught by her nose, shook the trap,
   shook three drops of bright blood into the air.

3. We camped out with a double sleeping bag,
   stars and the cold aphrodisiac.
   All night fur stroked my legs.
   As the sun came up, sharp teeth of a meadow mouse
   slit my bare toe.

4. If you don't want to crush a trapped
      mouse under your shoe
   cover trap and mouse with a shovel. Press firmly.

5. Our grey squirrel loves acorns.
   Our grey squirrel loves dog food.
   He drinks from the bird bath,
   scolds blue jays,
   leaps from branch to high branch of the oaks.
   He carried a mouse dead of poisoned grain

out of my reach, the range of my pebbles.
Holding the mouse in his tiny hands,
our grey squirrel ate first the ears,
then the whiskers, the feet, every morsel,
even the tail.

6. The latest in mouse control,
   the exterminator tells me,
   is this strip covered with
   powerful, pesticide-permeated
   soft glue and almost invisible steel needles.

7. *For Mousie, the Fast Woman*

   She was only a little animal
   trying to live by her wits.
   Why should she deserve such fur?

8. The musician returns from her tour.
   On her keyboard she finds mouse turds.
   She buys a small cage, but the spring is broken.
   She sits by the cage for hours, days, perfectly still.
   A large mouse runs in.
   She pulls a string.
   She leaves early next morning,
   drives to Vermont, releases the mouse.

9. Next week she catches a young mouse.
   It's Super Mouse, Super Ball, a bundle of electricity.
   Maddened, it careens off the cage walls.
   When she opens the cage door, it stiffens, catatonic.
   Her husband, a psychologist, has an explanation,

something about adolescent metabolism.
He offers to kill the mouse; it will not, he says, recover
She sits by the open cage. She still can see
a faint pulse, an occasional tremble.

10. We cut the dry corn stalks,
     stood them upright in shocks
     like a village of tepees across the field.
     Warm Saturdays in January we took the mutt,
     the feist, the terrier, and the twenty-two,
     threw down the shocks one by one,
     scattered the mice,
     cheered the dogs on.
     Horace, our hero, and Paul, whom I loved,
     took turns with the gun.
     None escaped, none.

11. On a Girl Scout walk, Diane,
     ten, found a shovel-nosed snake.
     As though illuminated from within,
     circles white and black
     down the length of its body gleamed.
     For her snake she built a glass house;
     laid a floor of sand, provided rock,
     plant, dish of water, a wide vent.
     Everything the book suggested.
     The snake buried itself, now and then
     emerged to soak its supple skin.
     Held gently, it curled round her wrist, her neck,
     explored her ear,

with its forked tongue tested her hair.
Once each month, the book said,
a snake needs food.
Round the terrarium,
cross-legged, silent, still,
the children sat in a circle,
rigid as the paralyzed mouse,
intent as the snake: intent.

12. When we built our house,
in rolls of fiberglass insulation
the mountain mice made their nests,
chewing the airy pink clouds,
stirring them with their clawed fingers.
One after another we found them,
sleeping. Their bodies broke in our fingers,
brittle as icicles, as ribbon candy.

13. Little mouse,
I was not ready to be a mother. Perhaps you knew.
The long months before birth you fought and twisted.
When I held you in my shaking hands,
you stiffened and kicked.
My milk shot out of your mouth.
When you stopped crying, it was for a moment
    only.
You slept, then, like a mouse on your father's
    breast.

CLOSEST TO VIRGO

In the Southern sky,
closest to Virgo,
lies Corvus. "Ca ca
ca," she calls.
"Daughter, I follow you.
I've got my black eye on your
bones, Daughter, eyebone,
earbone, ca, ca,
O bone of perfection,
dutiful bone, Daughter,
heartbone, Daughter,
ca, ca, ca."

MEDUSA

for Susan

We followed a dry watercourse over bleached and
    stained granite,
    heard a False-Hawk call from a white spruce and
from a broken fir the true hawk.
We came to a deep cut in the rock, stone carved and
    smoothed by water;
    from one tree to another
    across the cut, two rusted cables swung.

We came at last to a trickle of water,
    to a pool where fingerling
    brown trout swam.
You found a single blue feather,
    too pale for a jay's.
You spoke to black squirrels
    and they answered you.
Your face woke me;

that guttural groan
    repeated faster and faster was not crows' caw.
We heard the wail of young hungry for meat
    answered,
saw great dark birds rise into the sun's nimbus,
    white heads, the spread white fans of their tails
      shining.

We touched columbine, fireweed, Solomon's seal,
    a snake's track under horsetail fern.
At the trail's highest point, where water
    spills over the edge above,
    mist clung to the hairs on our fingers.
Mist made an aura around you.

The trunk of a sugar-pine wraps itself in snake scale
The branches, themselves trunks, twist
    upward against prevailing winds.
    Storm ripped out a heavy tongue.
    Now a mouth,
    caught in the grimace men most fear, most desir
    cries out

its compound of agony and pleasure.
From the stone to which all words turn,
with the curl of your tongue you called her.

The snakes unwind their sensuous bodies.
What can we do?
If she speaks to us, we are immortal.

THE FISH

Have you seen those gilded fish,
all azure and green-gold, rose and pale orange?
Once I touched silken scales;
the hum of their colors swayed for weeks
—does even now—behind my eyes, an odor clean
as new-mown alfalfa. That fish stays
just under the surface of everything,
of the shaking when I
eat sugar, close my eyes to news from Ethiopia,
spend no day in jail, keep silent,
keep silent. Once in the middle
of the night I got up,
knowing something was wrong,
saw the fish on the polished floor,
desiccated, eyes beginning to glaze.
It hardly struggled when I picked it up.
All I could think was *water,*
but the faucets hissed, not
a drop from any. Even with one hand
I could remove the tank lid,
reservoir, the prophets say,
when earthquake comes, or the bombs.
There was room, if I forced down the ball cock
just a bit, to slip the fish in. Among
the strange pipes and sockets,
in so small a space, the fish
wriggled its whole body,
waved its gills;
its color brightened. How could I
have gotten lost in the hall, straight, true,

bathroom to bedroom without a crook or detour?
I met no one, yet when I reached the bed
it was empty; I heard the rush of water.

Fish, how will you live in those
currents under the city?

This morning a crow waked me,
knocking at the window with his hard beak.
He wanted, from just inside the glass,
the small faceted sphere a friend
gave me, saying, "You can see
all sorts of things in this crystal,
past, future,
souls you didn't know
you'd killed."

AFTER AN ILLNESS,
ON OLD FORT TOWNSEND BEACH

When I curl south of a log
in the wind's lee at low tide,
squirm like a tired seal,
the sand keeps me warm.
Millsmoke spirals southeast
today, its acid tart in the nose.
Tumble of pebbles in backwash
and the small surf's hush
carry me down. At first I hear
only my own blood's beating.
My hands clench, unclench.

The biggest octopi
hunt in the Sound's canyons,
map the curves and limits
of its haunted water. The bell
of the ship under the waves
tilts this way and that.
Deep currents bring
its clear notes to me.
                From Marrowstone,
where on such sunny mornings the fogbank
often hangs, the foghorn's three-noted
melody calls me, and in the Straits' channels
ships' horns groan to each other.
                        To wake
here, a crow plodding along right at my feet,
is to swim up from the throat of the sea,
the dead skin washed off, the eyes open.

IV. THE KINGDOM

THE KINGDOM

CHARLES L. BROLEY, CHAMPION EAGLE BANDER, TALKS OF EAGLES: HARD TIMES

Nobody bothers crows—
a few boys, maybe, practicing to shoot tiger.
When the eagle dropped,
that big crow who for so long
had lorded it in the top branch of the fir
didn't even see him.
He felt those talons deep in his back.
Didn't give up; squawked and struggled
all the way across the straits.
Then he did more, I guess, than tickle
the eagle's shins. One blow
of the curved beak tore out his throat.
Lord, what I've seen on these climbs.
The young birds didn't
seem enthusiastic about crow meat,
but they ate it.
Fish were sparse that year,
even duck and guillemot,
and the old birds flew home often
with those jokesters
shrieking in their claws.

BROLEY TALKS: THE EYRIE (1)

It's the top of a tree, mostly,
the tallest near water. The two eagles
gather sticks and fallen branches. Sometimes
they tear off a special branch, even a big one.
Loosely they weave a floor twelve feet across.
They swoop low over the meadow,
seize vines in their talons,
rise trailing long brown streamers.
They take great tufts of grass,
moss, lichen, cattails, corn stalks.
Once I saw a nesting eagle take a funeral wreath.

The nest complete,
one eagle brings in its claws a sprig of fresh green
White pine's a favorite, placed in the nest
as if for decoration. We don't know
why eagles keep this custom,
or whether for them it has practical value,
but the evergreen branch is always there.
Eagles have repaired some nests
each spring for more than a hundred years,
till the tree breaks with the weight.

Besides young eagles, I've encountered in the nests
songbirds—a Baltimore oriole singing at dawn;
porcupine; a coachwhip snake who hissed at me—
an old timer, his shed skins
hung about as though in a closet;
a Great Horned Owl on its own eggs
and one of the eagles';
raccoons. Fierce as the eagles are,
they never fight the little masked bears,
but fly away and build, elsewhere, again.

REMEMBERING A CHILD WHO DIED (
WHOOPING COUGH: BAMAKO, MALI

A friend brought me, from Mexico,
a baby crow with a sea-serpent head.
Of black clay it's made,
with sheep's wool burnished to metal.
All night someone, someone blows
into the little slit under its feet.
All night, all night I hear its wail,
shrill as the breath of dying children.

BROLEY TALKS: THE STORM

When the storm ended,
the waves rocked down,
and rain dwindled to a green mist.
We saw the jagged post:
high on the cliff
where the granite broke
clean and quick down to the water,
the oldest pine's dead crown,
where the eagles had nested,
under the wind had fallen.

THE CROW-FEATHER

Once a crow lived all alone in a broken willow,
the tallest, where in summer the lake
backed over a low ridge into a gully.
That depth drew catfish, bluegill,
bass, and many turtles.
The crow stalked the shore,
pulling crawdads out of their mud castles.

Wrens and finches mobbed the crow;
I shouted and threw peach pits.
Sometimes an eagle flew over
from the wild canyons of San Saba County.
The crow didn't give up his perch easily;
he kept coming back,
cawed his outrage from a scrub oak,
neglected the opened mussels I brought for him.
When the eagle flew calmly away,
I thought the crow had frightened him.

He walked where he pleased.
He sampled peaches spread on the roof to dry.
He pecked the bell of my sister's trombone.
On the table under the chinaberry tree,
he stood on the Bible,
pulled and pulled—
till he squawked in fury—
at the red ribbon marking my father's place.

When he took something,
he always left a gift in return:

for a twist of taffy, an acorn;
for an ivory bead, a piece of pearly shell;
for the key to my hope chest, a nugget of fool's
 gold;
for my one shiny bangle, the leg bone of a skunk.

Crow the color of desire
and fear, when you brought me a feather
so black it glistened blue in the sun,
I kept it forever.
Where have you gone?
I have ripe ears of corn for you,
mangoes, apricots, abalone,
haunches of deer, high-smelling.

BROLEY TALKS: THE EYRIE (2)

Ton-and-a-half at least, John said.
Empty a long while; then,
DDT outlawed, the shooters fined,
the big white-tailed, white-headed
hawks came back.
They worked for weeks rebuilding.
We'd seen the young already out,
circling after the old birds,
up the canyon, out over the water
so far we lost them against the sky.
When they cried for meat, even I
wanted to scavenge and kill to bring it.
Now the old birds circled
and cried over empty space;
the young—from a bare tree—cried.

WHEN I FALL

When I fall into hell,
I remember: crow has been here.
When I want to fly beyond
reach of any eye:
eagle has been there.
If I want a nest,
two things are necessary:
a sprig of white pine;
crow's bones.
If, to tickle a lover,
I choose from my wings those feathers
black as a crow's,
though my lover leave me,
he shall leave me whole.

BROLEY TALKS:
INVESTIGATING THE CORE

Caught in a single band of the spectrum—
the air around us luminous—
we found the central mass of the nest,
huge, still glued to the biggest branch,
with an odor curiously clean.

Sticks and bones scattered all around,
John wrote, *and a great lump of humus:*
fine particles of decaying wood,
feathers, fur, earth, droppings.
Whole feathers, whole bones
of fish (90%), chicken, rat, muskrat,
rabbit, squirrel, raccoon.
A Clorox bottle, a long white candle.
An electric light bulb.
An old shoe, a family portrait (framed).
A fly swatter, a pair of pink panties.
Bones of duck, coot, plover, murre,
gull, grebe, crow.

THE NATURE OF LOVE

I've seen gulls and a single crow
mob, for hours, an eagle, each time
he came down to Aleck Bay to hunt.
He'd flap back to his tree,
watch till they scattered,
try again. At dusk,
we saw him hunched on the top branch, dark
against high cirrus turned gold and coral.
The crow made a last sweep downshore,
his black lost against dark forest,
caws resounding over the water.

North, where spent salmon
pile up in pools below the glacier's
crumbling cliff, the eagles
feed shoulder to shoulder,
the adolescents mobbed by crows,
gulls wheeling and snatching.
When, the salmon picked clean,
old eagles fall,
young crows pluck their sinews
like harpstrings,
gouge out those powerful eyes.

Between the Clorox bottle
and the pink panties, Crow,
easily your bones will rot.
Your shadow will show up, someday,
in the family portrait,
the frame gilded with your blood.
You were your own light bulb,

but you would have liked ours,
would have fought to tweak out
the worm-wick of that candle.
Plucking out your feathers,
the small eagles learn what they
need to know of the nature of power.

WAKING TO FOG

Working Late

How few times have I lain down with you
or risen to follow you into the light.
As I work, through the crack under the door
your sighs slip, eloquent as Orpheus' softest word.

The Struggle

All night we wrestled. I wanted
to climb the ladder, whether up
or into the dark, down, it didn't matter.
You would not let go of me.
At sunup, the hand with which you
grasped my hair was swollen, would not unclench.
When the moon's smoky and red lopsided circle
dropped behind the eroded
mountains west of our burning valley,
I'd kissed the hollow between thigh and groin.
The sinew shrank. All your life you'll limp.

The Cuckoo

How is it you so love the cuckoo's call,
in late afternoon echoed by some California bird
across the shadowed canyon?

When, lovers with children grown,
at Fontainebleau we followed the cuckoo,
its call beckoned to us

like the call of a lone Texas Comanche,
receding into tall straight oaks
first pruned while the Sun King postured,

beyond those preserved when the sixteenth
Louis died. Often—young,
seated on drought-twisted, prick-leaved

oak branches that had sheltered Quanah Parker,
we fell from history to kisses.
Now I was again awkward, fearful of surprise;

among my childhood's worshipped scrubs,
here grown higher than the courthouse tower,
by your fresh kisses

you brought me to desire as full
as, in the wooden oil derrick beyond the millet field,
the circle of the great wheel made of oak:

as full and ripe as yours.

Walking Into the Canyon

Today, careful of my strength, you led me
under fir, madrone, oaks so big
even from a child's-eye level I could not have

dreamt them. I led you where wild irises
thick as stars in the moon's dark, ivory to lavender
bloom with blue-eyed grass and wild onion.

Even in a small wind high branches grind together.
Standing where sun never reaches,
we heard, we thought, the cuckoo.

Could it be? you said. Could it? I said.
We still don't know, but your kiss
holds me as strongly as that clenched,

swollen hand, the hollow vulnerable to my lips.

Waking to Fog

When fog blows out the lights south around the bay,
fills the canyon with snow to reflect the moon,
rises white and luminous around the house,

I like to wake you with kisses,
to touch you gently, to feel you turn to me
with all your gifts ready,
our bodies risen out of sleep
like plums full of sweetness but not yet ripe.

While the seawind blew and the oaks budded—
pink, copper, orange, yellow-green—unable to
believe, I in any human love, you
in God, we longed for death.
It will find us. Now, even
in pain sometimes, we savor breath, sun, dark,
the touch of loved flesh waked from sleep.

CLIMBING THE CANYON TRAIL

Where the trail from the corral joins the trail
  to Shirley Lake,
coarse yellow-brown powder
and tiny bits of straw the horses could not digest
cover the dust shod hooves grind from weathered
  granite.
From those large loose brown marshmallows
the horses leave, from the few shiny ones
that look as if they'd dry hard as ebony,
a rich smell, clean as a field of alfalfa, rises.

One of those facts from childhood I didn't know I knew:
how different mule turds are,
firm, tightly packed,
a shining black surface like a thick skin,
a smell both more bitter and more sweet.

A mule, a neighbor told me when he rode one over
and tried to sell him to my father,
is a hybrid combining the best and worst
of horse and donkey, but sterile.
Perhaps, I thought, I was a hybrid:
Mother and Dad so different:
she, smaller than my friends, meek-voiced,
laughed only behind her hand at jokes he never saw,
whipped us only for broken laws
learned from Scotch-Irish Calvinists, but never,
once we were weaned, held us close;
he, taller than the doorframes, his speech a shout,
sang "When I was single my pockets would jingle"

and took me in his lap one second,
the next beat my sisters with sticks or straps
or his bare fists, pounded their heads on the floor.
"I'd never have a mule on my place," he yelled,
but he beat the horses, cursing their stubbornness.

Or maybe I was something worse than a mule—
"A whistlin' woman and a crowin' hen," he told me,
"always come to one bad end."

Yesterday in this noisy resort a carnival set up,
and a thousand cars
filled the macadammed cirque in high mountains.
All day a string of horses, heads down,
slouched as slowly as possible
back and forth past my window, toward the lake trail.
The pack mule, last in line, twitched his long ears
and every so often bucked. Last night,
just before dark, far up the slope, over the distorted
moon of a horseshoe in dust,
I saw a print with seven pads, like those of a cat.
The impossible animal that laid them down led me upward.
I heard him in every shadow.

A father can say he loves his daughters,
the saying fence and saddle, whip, harness,
iron bar dragged to learn the feel of the plow.
My brother taught me to milk a cow, to talk
to those sad animals, to calm their kicks.
"Contrary thing," my mother said,
driving her elbow into an impacted bag,

but Paul whispered in their ears,
rubbed their necks, cleaned and poulticed
their split and swollen teats.
He taught me to curry a horse,
to comb the forelock and polish the hooves,
to dig out screwworms from the furry hide.
He swung me up to the bare back
of that intelligent, dangerous animal,
whom he'd taught me when two years old
to pet and beware of. When I married,
perhaps it was for hands like his
and a whisper I remembered.

Today I climb up just a little way into the canyon, turn off at the first tiny creek. Farther up, I step on rounded boulders, through matted grass and willows, fireweed, wild parsnip, mountain goldenrod; make a short straight path where the water meanders under decaying roots and alder branches. Suddenly the creek spreads out; among large boulders of a moraine it has formed a bowl or womb. There's a flat stone for me to rest where the fetus would float. Bright yellow and orange columbine sway in sun, their scrolled center petals like Christmas ribbon candy, the yellow pistils hanging down like the long clapper of a cowbell. Here in this half-cave—earth, water, air, and vegetable life around me, while far above the fire of space burns—I feel in each cell the long loves, human and animal, that have brought me here.